AN ATTEMP'

THE BRECON BEAC(

or

THE SOUTHERN CAMBRIAN
MOUNTAINS

****

AN ARTISTIC IMPRESSION

BASED UPON

A SERIES OF ENGRAVINGS

IN FOUR PARTS

1. The Black Mountains

2. The Brecon Beacons

3. Fforest Fawr

4. The Black Mountain

DAVID S.YERBURGH

2004

I

PREFACE

CAMBRIA

On SCENES like these the eye delights to dwell;
Here loud CASCADES - and there the silent DELL,
MOUNTAINS of towering height - fantastic shape,
At whose broad base, terrific CHASMS gape:
HILLS, clothed in gayest verdure, smile serene,
Whilst rude and barren ROCKS, contrast the scene.
Varied by light and shade's perpetual change,
The enraptured ARTIST finds an endless range.

These are the words of introduction to the well known book *'Wales Illustrated in a Series of Views'*, a book of one hundred and sixty eight views of Wales, engraved on steel from original drawings by Henry Gastineau, c.1830. They also sum up satisfactorily in a few words the purpose of this present volume.

This small book has been designed to try to describe something of the diversity of the scenery, the places and the objects of interest that are to be found in the Brecon Beacons National Park, or in *'The Southern Cambrian Mountains'* as I have called them in this volume. These varied aspects of creation, that are so abundant in the National Park, have also been illustrated whenever possible by the skills of a variety of eighteenth and nineteenth century artists and engravers.

David S.Yerburgh.

****
ISBN 0 9535 6354 5

Published by
© Revd Canon David Yerburgh.
2 Mill Race Close, Mill Road, Salisbury, Wiltshire. SP2 7RX.

Printed by
The Baskerville Press Ltd., Salisbury, Wiltshire

THE BLACK MOUNTAIN TOUR No.6

LLANDOVERY, Y PIGWN & TRECASTLE

After visiting the Black Mountain (Bannau Sir Gaer) the tour returns to the busy market town of **Llandovery,** at the junction of three main roads and three rivers. The Welsh translation of Llandovery into English is *'The Church of many waters'* and an old saying states that one cannot leave the Church of St. Dingat without crossing water, which is absolutely true, as the church is surrounded by the rivers Tywi, Bran and Gwydderig. The Romans built a five-acre fort to defend the river and the site of this fort is near the car park. However, the remains of the castle that can be seen today are Norman and were built in the 13th century, and consist of an oval motte, a square bailey and some later masonry.

From Llandovery it is convenient to leave the main A40 and take the minor to the south and visit the Roman Fort and Camp established near the old Roman road. This ancient site is known as **Y Pigwn** and the Roman road crosses the hills and moors, via Trecastle, all the way to Y Gaer, near Brecon (see p.39). From here there are fine views to the south of the Black Mountain and the area below the extensive Usk reservoir.

Finally one comes to **Trecastle,** a former coaching village on the old Roman road from Y Pigwn called Mynydd Bach Trecastell. The castle, after which the village is named, is the early 12th century motte and bailey that can be seen on the north side of the main A40. It is the oldest motte and bailey fortification in the Brecon Beacons National Park and so it makes a fitting end to this tour, which began at Sennybridge.

'Llandovery Castle was situated on a rocky eminence, of moderate elevation, on the western bank of the Bran river. It seems never to have been a building of great extent. The present remains consist of a part of the keep, the site of the outer ward, and the trenches which surrounded the works. The first mention of it is about the year 1113, in the reign of Henry the first, when it was in the hands of Richard de Pons.'
T.Rees. 1815.

BIBLIOGRAPHY

A Tour through Momouthshire and Wales. H.P.Wyndham 1781.

Picturesque Guide through Wales & the Marches. J. Baker. 1795.

An Historical Tour in Monmouthshire. W.Coxe. 1801.

A Tour throughout South Wales & Monmouthshire. T.Barber. 1803.

The History of Brecknockshire. T.Jones. 1809.

The Principal Rivers of Wales. J.G.Wood. 1813.

The Beauties of South Wales. T. Rees. 1815.

The Beauties of Cambria. H.Hughes. 1823.

South Wales Illustrated. H.Gastineau. 1830.

The Beauties of Glyn Neath. W. W. Young 1835.

Wanderings in South Wales.T.Roscoe. 1837.

Black's Guide to South Wales. 1874.

Kilvert's Diary. 1870-1879.

Thorough Guides. South Wales. 1901.

Highways & Byways in South Wales. F.L.Griggs. 1903.

The Waterfalls of Wales. J.L.Jones. 1986.

Ordnance Survey Leisure Guide. Brecon Beacons & Mid Wales. 1989.

Castles of Wales. A. Reid. 1999.

The Brecon Beacons National Park Guide. R.Thomas & H.Williams. 2002.

INTRODUCTION

THE BRECON BEACONS NATIONAL PARK

or

THE SOUTHERN CAMBRIAN MOUNTAINS

When one looks at a map depicting the whole of Wales, or Cambria as it used to be known, it is quite usual to find written, almost diagonally over the whole map, the words *'The Cambrian Mountains'*. However to be more accurate *'The Cambrian Mountains'* are in fact the mountains and areas of high ground south of The Snowdonia National Park and north of The Brecon Beacons National Park.

In 1814-15 Thomas Compton, the drawing master at the Royal Military College at Woolwich, went on a tour of what we now call Snowdonia. The result of this tour was that he produced a set of thirty drawings of the area. In 1817 these thirty pictures were then reproduced as hand coloured aquatints, together with two pages of text for each engraving. These were then printed under the title *'The Northern Cambrian Mountains'* with the sub-title *' A tour through North Wales, describing the scenery and general characters of that romantic country.'*

At about the same time that Thomas Compton undertook his tour of North Wales, several books illustrated with engravings were also produced of South Wales. For example:-

'A Tour throughout South Wales' by J.T.Barber in 1803.
'The Scenery of South Wales' by B.II.Malkin in 1804.
'The Rivers of South Wales' by J.G.Wood in 1813.
'The Beauties of South Wales' by T.Rees in 1815.
'South Wales Illustrated' published by Jones & Co. 1830.
'Wanderings in South Wales' by T.Roscoe in 1844.

All these books covered the whole of South Wales, but as far as I can find out, no printed book of drawings was produced in the early or mid-nineteenth century which exclusively depicted the area now covered by The Brecon Beacons National Park, or *'The Southern Cambrian Mountains'*.

This present small volume is intended to complement my last book based upon Thomas Compton's tour of Snowdonia, which I titled *'An attempt to depict the Northern Cambrian Mountains'*. With this in mind I have titled this companion volume *'An attempt to depict the Brecon Beacons National Park'; with the sub title 'The Southern Cambrian Mountains'*. However, unlike the first book, which was illustrated by just one artist and writer, this volume is illustrated by several artists, engravers and writers, who were working at roughly the same time as Thomas Compton painted and wrote about his tour in Snowdonia.

The Brecon Beacons National Park falls into four distinct areas which from east to west are as follows;-

    1. The area known as 'The Black Mountains'
    2. The area known as 'The Brecon Beacons'
    3. The area known as 'Fforest Fawr'
    4. The area known as 'The Black Mountain'

These four areas of the National Park, for the purposes of this book, I have called collectively *'The Southern Cambrian Mountains'*. I have also attempted to create a tour of each of these four areas and they are summarized on the following four pages, with the ordnance survey map references of the main attractions that can be seen on the way. Where it has been possible these attractions have been illustrated by an eighteenth or nineteenth century engraving, which illustrates the many outstanding views and places of interest in this stunningly beautiful part of South Wales. Where no engraving has been available a black and white photograph has been used instead.

David S.Yerburgh

Salisbury

THE TOURS OF THE SOUTHERN CAMBRIAN MOUNTAINS

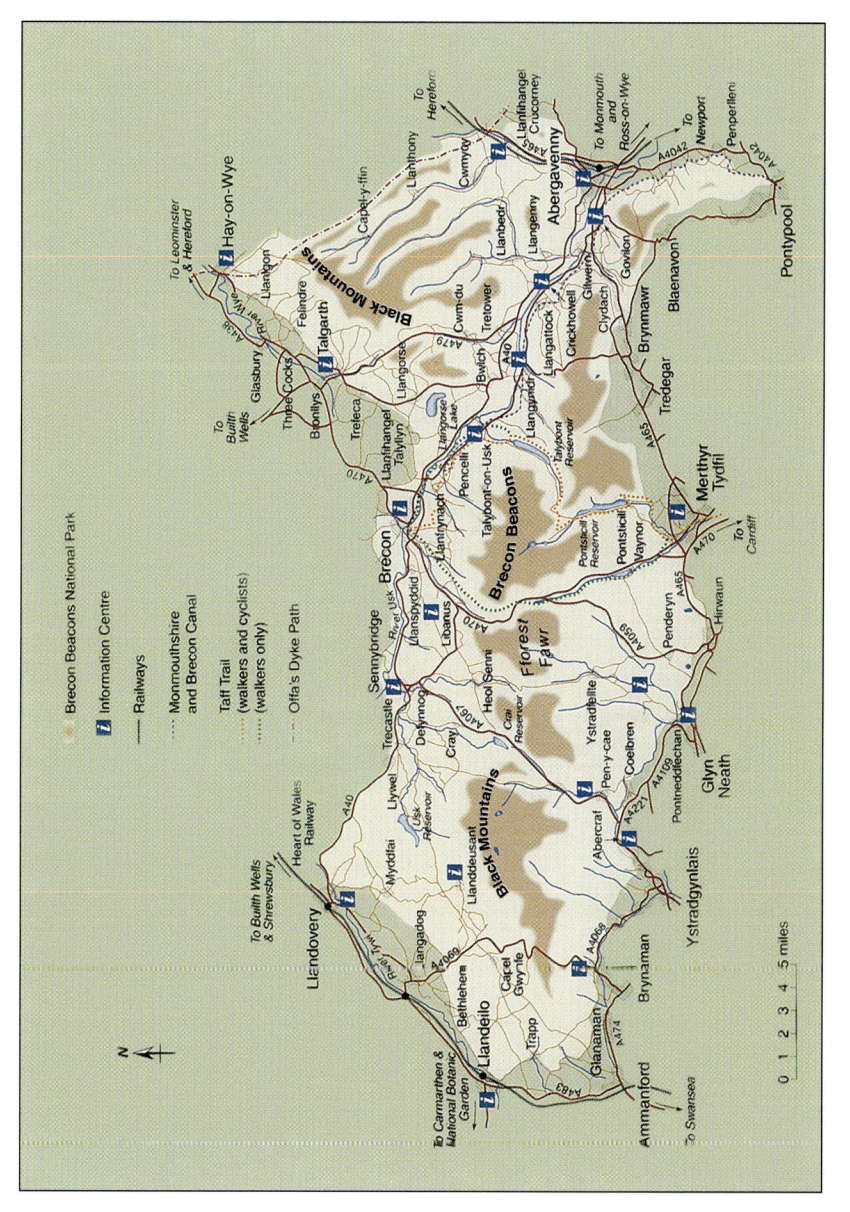

TOUR ONE THE BLACK MOUNTAINS

Starting point – Brecon

This includes the area on the east of the A40 from Brecon to Abergavenny, to the west of the A465 and Gospel Pass from Abergavenny to Hay-on-Wye, and to the south of the A438/A470 from Hay-on-Wye to Brecon.

No.	View	OS reference	Page
1.	BRECON CATHEDRAL	OS 160, 045 290	8 & 9
2.	LLANGORSE LAKE	OS 161, 130 265	10 & 11
3.	TRETOWER CASTLE	OS 161, 185 212	12 & 13
4.	CRICKHOWELL	OS 161, 218 182	14 & 15
5.	THE SUGAR LOAF &	OS 161, 274 188	16 & 17
5.	THE SKIRRID MOUNTAINS	OS 161, 331 182	16 & 17
6.	ABERGAVENNY	OS 161, 299 140	18 & 19
7.	PARTRISHOW CHURCH	OS 161, 279 224	20 & 21
8.	CWMYOY CHURCH	OS 161, 299 233	22 & 23
9.	LLANTHONY PRIORY	OS 161, 288 280	24 & 25
10.	CAPEL-Y-FFIN	OS 161, 255 316	26 & 27
11.	HAY BLUFF	OS 161, 244 366	28 & 29
12.	HAY-ON-WYE	OS 161, 228 422	30 & 31
13.	BRONLLYS CASTLE &	OS 161, 150 347	32 & 33
13.	TALGARTH WATERFALL	OS 161, 174 326	32 & 33

TOUR TWO THE BRECON BEACONS

Starting point – Brecon

This includes the area west of the A40/A4042 from Brecon to Pontypool, north of the A4043/B4248/A465 from Pontypool to Merthyr Tydfil and east of the A470 from Merthyr Tydfil to Brecon.

No.	View	OS reference	Page
1.	BRECON CASTLE & Y GAER	OS 160, 045 290	36 & 37
2.	TALYBONT-ON-USK	OS 161, 114 229	38 & 39
3.	LLANGYNIDR BRIDGE &	OS 161, 153 203	40 & 41
3.	LLANGATTOCK CHURCH	OS 161, 211 179	40 & 41
4.	GILWERN &	OS 161, 250 149	42 & 43
4.	THE CLYDACH GORGE	OS 161, 231 134	42 & 43
4.	GOVILON &	OS 161, 270 133	42 & 43
4.	THE BLORENGE	OS 161, 270 118	42 & 43
5.	PONTYPOOL &	OS 171, 295.005	44 & 45
5.	BLAENAVON	OS 161, 238 089	44 & 45
6.	MERTHYR TYDFIL	OS 160, 043 074	46 & 47
6.	PONTSTICILL	OS 160, 063 121	46 & 47
7.	STOREY ARMS &	OS 160, 982 203	48 & 49
7.	FFWDGRECH WATERFALL	OS 160, 020 265	48 & 49

TOUR THREE FFOREST FAWR

Starting point – Brecon

This includes the area west of the A470 from Brecon to Merthyr Tydfil, north of the A465/A4109/A4221 from Merthyr Tydfil to Abercraf, east of the A4067 from Abercraf to Sennybridge, and then south of the A40 from Sennybridge to Brecon.

No.	View	OS reference	Page
1.	BRECON BRIDGE &	OS 160, 044 285	52 & 53
1.	BRECON FRIARY &	OS 160, 043 284	52 & 53
1.	LIBANUS	OS 160, 978 262	52 & 53
2.	PONTNEDDFECHAN &	OS 160, 911 077	54 & 55
2.	THE FALLS ON PYRDDIN	OS 160, 896 093	54 &.55
2.	THE FALLS ON NEDD &	OS 160, 903 097	54 & 55
3.	CRAIG Y DDINAS &	OS 160, 915 081	56 & 57
3.	BWA MAEN	OS 160, 916 082	56 & 57
4.	COELBREN &	OS 160, 850 117	58 & 59
4.	HENRHYD FALL	OS 160, 854 120	58 & 59
5.	FALLS ON MELLTE &	OS 160, 925 109	60 & 61
5.	FALLS ON HEPSTE	OS 160, 930 100	60 & 61
6.	PORTH YR OGOF &	OS 160, 927 122	62 & 63
6.	YSTRADFELLTE &	OS 160, 930 135	62 & 63
6.	MAEN LLIA	OS 160, 925 193	62 & 63

TOUR FOUR THE BLACK MOUNTAIN

Starting point – Sennybridge

This includes the area west of the A4067 from Sennybridge to Abercraf, North of the A4068/A4069/A474 from Abercraf to Glanaman, and east of the minor road from Glanaman to Llandeilo, and south of the A40 from Llandeilo to Sennybridge.

No.	View	OS reference	Page
1.	SENNYBRIDGE &	OS 160, 922 284	66 & 67
1.	DEFYNNOG &	OS 160, 925 279	66 & 67
1.	MAEN MAWR	OS 160, 852 207	66 & 67
2.	DAN YR OGOF &	OS 160, 840 160	68 & 69
2.	CRAIG Y NOS &	OS 160, 845 155	68 & 69
2.	SAITH MAEN	OS 160, 835 154	68 & 69
3.	RIVER LOUGHOR &	OS 159, 675 179	70 & 71
3.	CARREG CENNEN	OS 159, 668 191	70 & 71
4.	LLANDEILO CHURCH &	OS 159, 629 223	72 & 73
4.	DINEFWR PARK	OS 159, 615 225	72 & 73
5.	CARN GOCH &	OS 159, 685.242	74 & 75
5.	LLANDDEUSANT	OS 160, 777 246	74 & 75
5.	THE BLACK MOUNTAIN	OS 160, 805 220	74 & 75
6.	LLANDOVERY CASTLE	OS 160, 770 341	76 & 77
6.	Y PIGAN & ROMAN ROAD	OS 160, 828 313	76 & 77
6.	TRECASTLE	OS 160, 883 290	76 & 77

TOUR ONE

THE BLACK MOUNTAINS

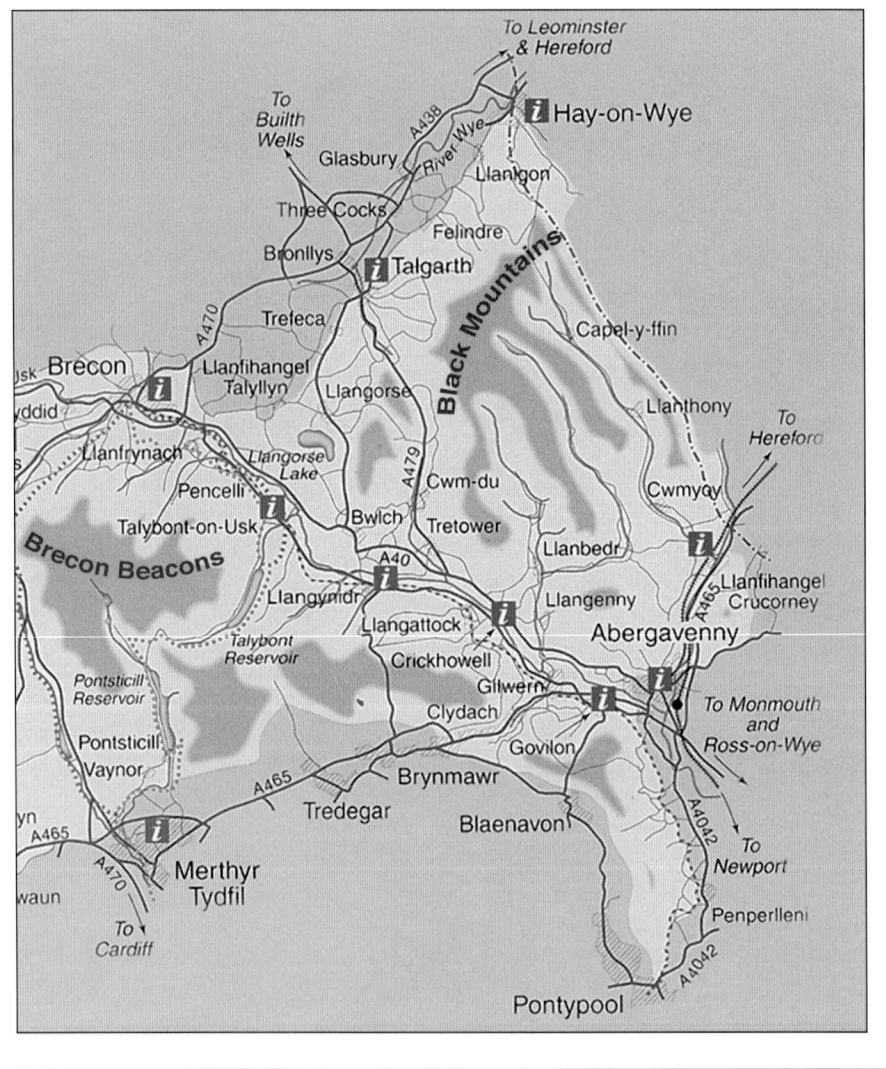

TOUR ONE

THE BLACK MOUNTAINS

BRECON

LLANGORSE

TRETOWER

CRICKHOWELL

SUGAR LOAF & SKIRRID FAWR

ABERGAVENNY

PARTRISHOW

CWMYOY

LLANTHONY

CAPEL Y FFIN

THE GOSPEL PASS

HAY ON WYE

BRONLLYS

TALGARTH

THE BLACK MOUNTAINS TOUR No.1

BRECON CHURCH

(Brecon Cathedral)

Steel engraving

Drawn by D. Cox & Engraved by W. Radclyffe

c. 1837

THE BLACK MOUNTAINS TOUR No.1

BRECON

The ancient town of **Brecon** gave its name to the former county of Brecknockshire or Brycheiniog, but is now part of the county of Powys. It is beautifully situated in the valley of the River Usk and looks up on one side towards the Black Mountains and Waun Fach (811m) and on the other side to the Brecon Beacons and Pen y Fan (886m).

Because of this central position, Brecon has also been chosen as the starting point for three of the four of the tours of the *'Southern Cambrian Mountains'*. The starting point for this first tour of the Black Mountains is **Brecon Cathedral.**

The Church of St. John the Evangelist began its life as a Benedictine Priory and was founded by Bernard of Newmarch at the close of the 11th century, as a cell of the Benedictine monastery of Battle in Sussex. Little of the original Priory Church remains today, except for parts of the nave wall immediately west of the crossing, but many of the domestic buildings attached to the church survived the Dissolution and are still in use today as diocesan offices. After the Reformation the priory church was virtually rebuilt and it became the parish church of Brecon, which was then carefully restored by Sir Gilbert Scott in the nineteenth century. In 1923 it was chosen as the cathedral church of the Diocese of Swansea and Brecon.

After visiting the well cared for cathedral it is worth while spending some time visiting the excellent craft centre housed in the sensitively restored building in the cathedral close.

'Few towns surpass Brecknock in picturesque beauties: the magnificent range of mountain scenery, on the southern side of the town form, in many points of view, the most beautiful, rich and varied outline imaginable.'
Sir Richard Hoare. 1806.

THE BLACK MOUNTAINS TOUR No.2

BRECKNOCK MERE : LLANGORSE POOL

Copper Engraving
Thomas Jones

Six views of South Wales

c. 1775

Reproduced by permission of Llyfrgell Genedlaethol Cymru
The National Library of Wales

THE BLACK MOUNTAINS TOUR No.2

LLANGORSE LAKE

Llangorse Lake, which can be approached from many minor roads south east of Brecon, is one and a half miles wide and the largest natural lake in South Wales. It is well placed to view **Mynydd Llangorse (609m) and Mynydd Troed (609m),** which lie to the west of the A479 and in front of the Black Mountains.

At the north west side of the lake there is a man-made island or crannog, known as Bwlch. This island has been built from a large heap of stones and is thought to have been an Iron Age settlement. In 1925 a dug-out canoe was discovered dating back to AD 800 which can now be seen in Brecon Museum.

Giraldus Cambrensis is supposed to have visited Llangorse Lake on his tour of Wales and claimed that the birds here only sang to the true ruler of the principality. He also considered that the water of the lake had magical powers in that at times it appeared green and at other times it appeared to be tinged with blood red veins. In actual fact the water only looked red because the River Llynfi flows into the lake over red sandstone, which at times can leave a trail of discolouration!

The village of Llangorse consists simply of a few cottages built around the Norman church dedicated to St Paulinus with 6th century origins. Llangorse, on the village side of the lake, has now become popular site for visitors, and water sports. On the other side of the lake, at **Llangasty Talyllyn,** an area has been set aside as a wild life reserve for the rich natural life and the many species of birds that thrive in this delightful quiet part of the lake.

'I strolled on the banks of Llangorse lake, saw the old inscribed stone in its charming little church, and finally breasted the ascent of Mynydd Troed. It stands out from this group of the Black mountains, and looks right up the valley facing Brecon, nine miles away.'
A.G.Bradley. 1903.

THE BLACK MOUNTAINS TOUR No.3

TRETOWER CASTLE

Soft ground etching

Drawn and etched by J.G.Wood

c. 1811

THE BLACK MOUNTAINS TOUR No.3

TRETOWER CASTLE

From Llangorse Lake it is only a short distance along the A40 to Tretower Castle and Court, which look towards **Pen Cerrig-calch (701m)** and the distinctive flat topped **'Table Mountain'** near Crickhowell.

Tretower Castle began its life as a twelfth century motte. The exact date of this early defence is unknown, but it was originally founded by a Norman knight called Picard, and it has been established that the Picards were in the district by 1106. The Welsh then captured this Norman stronghold in 1233, but it soon reverted back to the English when the uprising was crushed. It was probably at this time that the bailey was added, with a stone surrounding wall with three small towers, and a tall round central keep. In 1404 it became a fortified castle for Henry IV against the attacks of Owain Glyndwr. Shortly after this the castle passed into the hands of Sir Roger Vaughan.

The residential potential of Tretower Castle was greatly increased by the building of a **manor house** in the fourteenth century. However the Vaughans rebuilt this and created a new fortified manor house, which then replaced the castle as their family home. Over the years many alterations have been made but the original manor has survived. In recent years CADW has completed a wonderful restoration of this building and it is open to the public in the summer months.

'Tre-twr, literally the Town of the Tower is to be ascribed to an early period of the Norman occupation of the county, when the new settlers were obliged to trust their security to stone walls. It seems never to have held any considerable rank as a fortress, and is to be regarded as a castellated mansion.'
T.Rees. 1815.

THE BLACK MOUNTAINS TOUR No.4

CRICKHOWELL

Soft ground etching

Drawn and etched by J. G. Wood

c. 1811

THE BLACK MOUNTAINS TOUR No.4

CRICKHOWELL

From Tretower the tour continues southwards to the attractive small town of **Crickhowell,** built on the edge of a hill looking towards the Sugar Loaf Mountain (596m). It takes its name from the ancient Iron-Age fortress, **Crug Hywel** or Howell's Fort, on the summit of the **Table Mountain (451m)** north east of the town.

The River Usk is very wide at Crickhowell and is crossed by an amazing **ancient and narrow arched bridge,** which today can cause considerable traffic hold ups. It is well worth finding time to stop and view this beautiful bridge, which is known to have been in existence in 1538. The bridge was rebuilt in 1706 with local stone and is curious in that it has thirteen arches on one side and twelve on the other, but this was the result of further restoration work done in 1830.

On the south side of the town, close to the A40 in a public park are the remains of **Alisby's Castle,** which was built in 1272 by Sir Grimbald Pauncefort. It passed into several different hands until it eventually came into the possession of Roger Mortimer. Its name derives from his ally Alisby, who was given the castle as a thank offering for Mortimer's release from the Tower of London. Today little remains of the castle other than the gatehouse tower, with curtain wall and the portcullis gate.

The 14th century church at Crickhowell, dedicated to St. Edmund, has undergone various restorations, but it has an interesting lancet window at the west-end and a font bearing the date 1688.

'The situation of Crickhowel, upon the side of a hill on the north-east bank of the Usk, is beautiful in extreme. The views either up or down are of so pleasing, so romantic, and so picturesque a character, that no one, however indifferent to the charms of nature, can fail to be sensible of their attractions.' J.G. Wood. 1813.

THE BLACK MOUNTAINS TOUR No.5

Abergavenny, and Sugar Loaf Mountain, from the Monmouth Road.

THE SUGAR LOAF AND SKIRRID MOUNTAIN

Steel engraving

Engraved by Newman & Co. & published by C.Denton, Abergavenny

c. 1870

16

THE BLACK MOUNTAINS TOUR No.5

SUGAR LOAF & SKIRIDD MOUNTAIN

After leaving Crickhowell on the A40 and just before Abergavenny there is a turning on the left, which takes one to a good car park half the way up the **Sugar Loaf Mountain (596m),** now in the care of the National Trust.

The Sugar Loaf Mountain takes its name from the conical shape of its distinctive summit. From the car park there is a zig-zag path to the top, from which there are superb views across the Bristol Channel in one direction and to the Malvern Hills in the other direction.

To the east of the Sugar Loaf and just off the A465 is another distinctive mountain, also in the care of the National Trust, known as **Skirrid Fawr (486m)** or 'The Holy Mountain'. The origin of this alternative title is due to an ancient legend that the ridge of the mountain was formed at the time of the Christ's crucifixion. Close to the summit are the remains of a small medieval chapel dedicated to St Michael, where secret masses used to be held by Roman Catholics during their persecution in the seventeenth century. The surrounding soil was considered to be holy and was often scattered by local farmers on their failed crops!

To the south of Skirrid Fawr there is a third smaller mountain called **Skirrid Fach (249m),** or 'Little Holy Mountain'. This makes an easy short walk from the town of Abergavenny.

'On approaching Abergavenny, the tourist's attention is involuntarily arrested by the singular beauty and variety of interest which the spot embraces, particularly in its encircling hills. To the right the elegant smooth cone of the Sugar-loaf, the highest of the Monmouthshire, mountains presents itself. Eastward of this mountain is the Great Skyridd, an object of considerable interest.'
J.T. Barber. 1803.

THE BLACK MOUNTAINS TOUR No.6

ABERGAVENNY

Steel engraving

Drawn by H. Gastineau and engraved by T. H. Shepherd

c. 1830

THE BLACK MOUNTAINS TOUR No.6

ABERGAVENNY

Abergavenny is a busy market town and could well be described as the principal southern entrance to the Black Mountains, and to the many places of interest in this delightful part of the National Park. It also makes a convenient starting place to walk to the Sugar Loaf, Skirrid Fawr and Skirrid Fach. (See previous page).

As well as being a busy tourist and shopping centre the town also has several buildings of historical interest. The first of these is **Abergavenny Castle.** The result of the ravages of the Parliamentary forces in 1645 has meant that today there are only a few remains. These remains simply consist of two towers, one round and the other polygonal, and a gate with a substantial barbican. The traditional motte and bailey were founded in the eleventh century, but the principal ruins belong to the thirteenth and fourteenth centuries. In later centuries this castle has had various additions made to it, including a hunting lodge which now houses an excellent local museum.

St. Mary's Priory, which is now the local parish church, was originally a Benedictine priory founded by Hamelin de Ballon, who also owned the castle. This priory was a cell to the Benedictine Abbey at Le Mans in France. It continued, after the suppression of the 'alien' priories, as a small independent priory and the burial place, with some splendid existing tombs, of several previous owners of the castle. Of particular interest is the huge 15th century wooden carving once the base of a Jesse tree. Today most of the church has been rebuilt, but it has a fourteenth century tower, presbytery, side aisles and Lady Chapel. In the choir there are some of the original priory stalls, with the carving of a mitre on the prior's stall.

'This town and its environs have strong claims on the traveller's attention. Its castle and delightful terrace, over looking the rich vale of Usk, its church abounding in costly sculptured tombs, and its beautifully variegated mountains, all conspire to render this place particularly attractive.'
South Wales Illustrated. 1830.

THE BLACK MOUNTAINS TOUR No.7

PARTRISHOW CHURCH

Blank and white photograph

Taken by the author

c. 2004

THE BLACK MOUNTAINS TOUR No.7

PARTRISHOW CHURCH

From Abergavenny the tour continues along the A465 to Llanfihangel Crucorney, where one turns left and then with some careful map reading one eventually comes to the hamlet of **Partrishow,** which looks up at **Partrishow Hill (466m)** in the foreground, and **Crug Mawr (550m)** in the distance.

Partrishow is really just a collection of farms and scattered houses, but it has a remarkably fine, small church, which is full of interest. This **church is dedicated to St. Issui** (see below). The church is thought to go back to the eleventh century and was founded by a wealthy pilgrim who was cured of his leprosy after drinking of the water from the well below the church. The font in the present church probably goes back to this first church.

The church is much the same today as it was in at the close of the Middle Ages, but with the addition of a thirteenth century chapel built on to the west wall. This extension acted as an oratory with a priest's room above it. The inside of the church is dominated by the superbly carved oak rood screen which dates back to the late fifteenth century and is considered to be one of the finest carved screens in Wales. The original access to the screen is through the doorway to the north. The chancel is Elizabethan and has replaced an earlier, narrower one, but the east window is thought to have come from the original chancel.

During restoration work in 1909 various ancient wall paintings were discovered which include a 'doom' figure of a skeleton with a scythe and an hour-glass and spade, a large Royal Coat of Arms, the Creed, Lord's Prayer and Commandments.

'Partricio; so called from a saint of the name of Ishaw, or as others, Ishow, of whom nothing is known, save from the tradition of the neighbourhood, where it is stated that he was a holy man, who led a religous life in this retired spot and had his little oratory upon the bank of a small rivulet called Nant Mair or Mary's Brook which runs at the bottom of the hill on which the church is built.'
Theophilus Jones. 1809.

THE BLACK MOUNTAINS TOUR No.8

CWMYOY CHURCH

Black and white photograph

Taken by Diana Coleridge

c. 2004

THE BLACK MOUNTAINS TOUR No.8

CWMYOY CHURCH

After visiting Partrishow church one returns to the Vale of Ewyas. On reaching the main road turn right almost immediately over the River Honddu. This eventually brings one to the small village of **Cwmyoy,** which nestles at the foot of **Hatterrall Hill (531m)** on one side and **Twyn y Gaer (426m),** the site of an Iron Age fort, on the other.

St. Martin's Church at Cwmyoy is particularly curious because it appears to be leaning in all directions, and one speculates on why on earth it has not fallen down! The cause of the extraordinary shape of the church is due to subsidence over the years. Apparently the church had been built below the site of an old landslide, and diagrams inside the church porch explain the reasons for the remarkable angles of the tower, walls and roof.

The origins of this church are obscure, but it is more than likely that there was a church here before the Norman Conquest. After the Norman Conquest the church came under the jurisdiction of the Priory at Llanthony. This historic link is still preserved today, as the churches at Llanthony and Cwmyoy both share the same parish priest.

The interior is simple and preserves much of the ancient features and atmosphere of the original medieval church. There are steps to a rood loft, but unlike Partrishow, this has now disappeared. The ninth or tenth century stone cross, now inside the church, is thought to have originally been a cross from the Pilgrim's Way to St. David's.

'Immediately to the left of the road rises the Gaer, a huge rocky hill crowned with an ancient encampment. On the opposite side of the river, fearfully hanging on a steep cliff, and beneath a menacing hill bristled with innumerable craigs, is the romantic village of Cwmjoy.'
J.T.Barber. 1803.

LLANTHONY ABBEY

Black & white aquatint

Drawn by J.Wathen & engraved by J.Bluck

c. 1795

THE BLACK MOUNTAINS TOUR No.9

LLANTHONY PRIORY

Having visited the unique church at Cwmyoy one returns to the main road along the Vale of Ewyas. Then one travels along this road for about five miles to **Llanthony village and the Priory.** Llanthony is beautifully situated between **Bal Mawr (607m)** on one side, and **Loxidge Tump (604m)** on the other.

The founders of the great monastic communities seem to have had the remarkable knack of discovering the most peaceful and beautiful places for the building of their monasteries, and Llanthony Priory was no exception to this principle. In the twelfth century the land belonged to the Lord of Ewyas, and it was one of his retainers, William de Lacey, who discovered the remains of a sixth century hermitage dedicated to St. David. This was Llanthony, a corruption of 'Llan-Dewi-Nant-Honddu' or 'the Church of St. David on the River Honddu'. William de Lacey settled there and rebuilt the cell and established a small monastic community in 1108. Legend says that the small parish church, dedicated to St. David, stands on the site of this first community church.

A permanent church and priory of Augustinian Canons was finally established at Llanthony in 1118, largely due to the generosity of Hugh de Lacey. The Priory Church was built between 1180 and 1230 and became one of the great medieval buildings of Wales. The priory was then devastated by Owain Glyndwr in 1399 causing it to become almost abandoned for fifty years, the majority of the canons going to a new foundation in Gloucester, called Llanthony Secunda. The ruins of the church and priory that survive today date back to the early thirteenth century and part of the priory buildings have been converted into a hotel.

'In the deep gloomy vale of Ewias, encircled by the barren summits of the Black mountains, but enjoying some degree of local cultivation, and enlivened by the crystalline Hondy, is situated the ruin of Llanthony Abbey.'
J.T.Barber. 1803.

THE BLACK MOUNTAINS TOUR No.10

CAPEL-Y-FFIN, NANT HONDDU

Watercolour

By Arthur Miles

c. 1930

Reproduced by permission of Llyfrgell Genedlaethol Cymru
The National Library of Wales

THE BLACK MOUNTAINS TOUR No.10

CAPEL-Y-FFIN

From Llanthony the tour continues up the Vale of Ewyas to **Capel-y-ffin,** a tiny hamlet in the heart of the Black Mountains. To the west, in the distance, is **Waun Fach (801m),** the highest mountain in the Black Mountains range. To the east, Offa's Dyke continues on its way separating Wales from England, and behind the dyke is **Black Hill (640m).**

Capel-y-ffin, although only a hamlet, has three churches in the parish. The first are the remains of **Llanthony Monastery,** built by Joseph Leycester Lyne. He felt that he had been called to the monastic life and founded a monastery in the Gothic Revival style in 1870. He set himself up as the Abbot, taking the name of Father Ignatius. The monastic life continued to thrive in the unfinished church and monastery until his death in 1908, when he was buried in the choir of the abbey. Sadly, after Father Ignatius's death, the numbers joining the community never grew and by 1916 it was empty and began to fall into disrepair. In 1924 the abbey was acquired by Eric Gill, the artist and engraver, who set up his workshops here and lived in the domestic buildings.

The other two churches are very close to the monastery. The first is the tiny white washed **parish church of St. Mary,** which has been a place of worship since 1762. The simplicity of the building both outside and inside is very appealing, especially the modern clear east window engraved so appropriately with the words *'I will lift up mine eyes unto the hills.'* The third church is behind St. Mary's churchyard. It is the small local **Baptist church,** which was once a schoolhouse.

'I remembered the old chapel short stout and boxy with its little bell turret (the whole building reminded one of an owl), the quiet peaceful chapel yard shaded by seven great solemn yews, the chapel house, a farm house over the way, and the great Honddu brook crossing the road and crossed in turn by the stone foot bridge.'
F.Kilvert. 1870.

BLACK MOUNTAINS TOUR No.11

WINTER AND THE BLACK MOUNTAINS

Photograph

Original coloured photograph by Ruth Hargest

Reproduced by kind permission of Ruth Hargest

THE BLACK MOUNTAINS TOUR No.11

THE GOSPEL PASS

The road from Capel-y-ffin to Hay-on-Wye, commonly known as **the Gospel Pass,** must be the most dramatic public road in the whole of the Black Mountains area of the National Park. The road is extremely narrow and great care must be taken if one is driving. Half way between Capel-y-ffin and Hay there is a parking place, which marks the start of two walks. The one on the left hand side of the road goes to **Twmpa or Lord Hereford's Knob (690m),** and the other on the right to **Hay Bluff (677m).**

The Evangelists' Pass or Bwlch-yr-Efengyl or the Gospel Pass as it is called today traces its name back to ancient folk law. This states that St Peter and St Paul visited the Black Mountains early in the first century when they walked up through the Honddu valley passing the future site of Llanthony Priory. Their purpose was to spread the gospel to the ancient Britons who were populating the area. Tradition also says this was at the request of Caradoc, the Welsh prince being held prisoner in Rome. However a more likely explanation of the title 'Gospel Pass' goes back to the beginning of the twelfth century when during the third crusade Giraldus Cambrensis, then Archdeacon of Brecon, travelled through the Vale of Ewyas, preaching and raising money for the crusade.

Pen-y-Beacon or Hay Bluff, the most northern of the Black Mountains, rises above the Offa's Dyke Path, which here reaches its highest point on its one hundred and sixty eight mile journey through the length of Wales. From Hay Bluff there are wonderful views over the town of Hay-on-Wye to the Wye Valley, and across to the hills of the Radnor Forest and Mynydd Eppynt.

'We rode by the nearest road, from the Hay to Abergavenny, that we might repeat our visit to the ruins of Llantony. The track over the mountains was intricate and boggy, 'till it brought us to the source of the Hodney, near Chapel y Fine situated in the very inmost recess of the Vale of Ewyas.'
H.P.Wyndham. 1781.

THE BLACK MOUNTAINS TOUR No.12

HAY

Steel engraving

Drawn by D. Cox and engraved by W. Radclyffe

c. 1837

THE BLACK MOUNTAINS TOUR No.12

HAY-ON-WYE

Having successfully negotiated the breath taking Gospel Pass one begins the gentle descent to the attractive town of **Hay-on-Wye**. The Hay, as it used to be called, is a border town in more ways than one. It is on the national border of Wales and England, on the border of the Brecon Beacons National Park and on the county borders of Powys, Hereford and Worcester. From the town there are superb views of the Black Mountains looking up to **Rhos Dirion (713m), Twmpa (690m), and Hay Bluff (677m).**

Since Hay is a border town it is not surprising to find it has a **castle**. Originally there was a castle near the parish church where there are still traces of a motte. In about 1200 a Norman castle was built on the site of the present castle in the centre of the town. Today only part of the walls and a thirteenth century gateway survive of the Norman castle, mainly due to the fact that in the seventeenth century a large mansion was built within its walls. In Victorian days this mansion was used as a vicarage for the Vicar of Hay, but in more recent years two fires have considerably damaged the building.

Today Hay-on-Wye is famous as a town of second hand books and people come from far and wide to look at the vast number of bookshops that can be found, many of which specialize in a variety of subjects. The creator of this interest in books was the great character Richard Booth, the owner of Hay Castle, who set himself up as 'The King of Hay', and declared Hay an independent town.

'The town of Hay is pleasantly situated on the rising bank of the Wye, and, from the vestiges of a Roman camp near the church, appears to have been of ancient origin. The manor of Hay was given by Bernard Newmarch to Sir Phillip Walwyn, who probably, built the castle, of which little remains but a gateway, a dwelling house having been erected out of the ruins's materials.' T.Roscoe. 1837.

THE BLACK MOUNTAINS TOUR No.13

BRONLLYS CASTLE

Wood engraving

Drawn and engraved by H.Hughes

c. 1823

THE BLACK MOUNTAINS TOUR No.13

BRONLLYS CASTLE & TALGARTH

From Hay-on-Wye the tour continues in a south-west direction to Bronllys. Just outside the village, on the A479 beside the River Llynfi, is the mid-thirteenth century **Bronllys Castle.** From the keep of the castle there are superb views of the Black Mountains, **Rhos Dirion (713m), Waun Fach (810m) and Pen y Gadair Fawr (800m).** Bronllys Castle was first established with a motte and bailey by Richard fitz Pons in the late 11th century; and in the 13th century the impressive tower was added by Walter de Clifford 111. The tower has recently been restored by CADW and there is now good access to the top, which clearly shows the signs of its former use as a residence.

About a mile from Bronllys Castle is the small town of **Talgarth.** This also had a castle built in 1088, but the motte and bailey have not survived. The curious thirteenth century tower, near the town bridge, was once a look-out post or possibly a prison. It has now been converted into a private dwelling.

South east of Talgarth, near the local hospital, is an attractive nature reserve, following the course of the River Ennig. At one point the river divides into two streams and forms a pair of delightful cascades, known as **Pwll-y-Wrach** or the Witch's Pool. The waterfall makes a good return point for this easy walk and an equally good place to end a tour of the Black Mountains.

'Bronllys is a small village, situated seven miles from Brecon on the road to Hay. The only remains of the castle is a lofty circular tower, placed on a moderately elevated site, on the banks of the Llynfi, and imparting much picturesque beauty to the surrounding scenery.'

H.Hughes. 1823.

'Tal-garth means literally the front of the hill, and the name is in this instance derived from the situation of this place, at one of the ends of the Black Mountains, which stretch into Herefordshire.'

T.Rees. 1815.

TOUR TWO

THE BRECON BEACONS

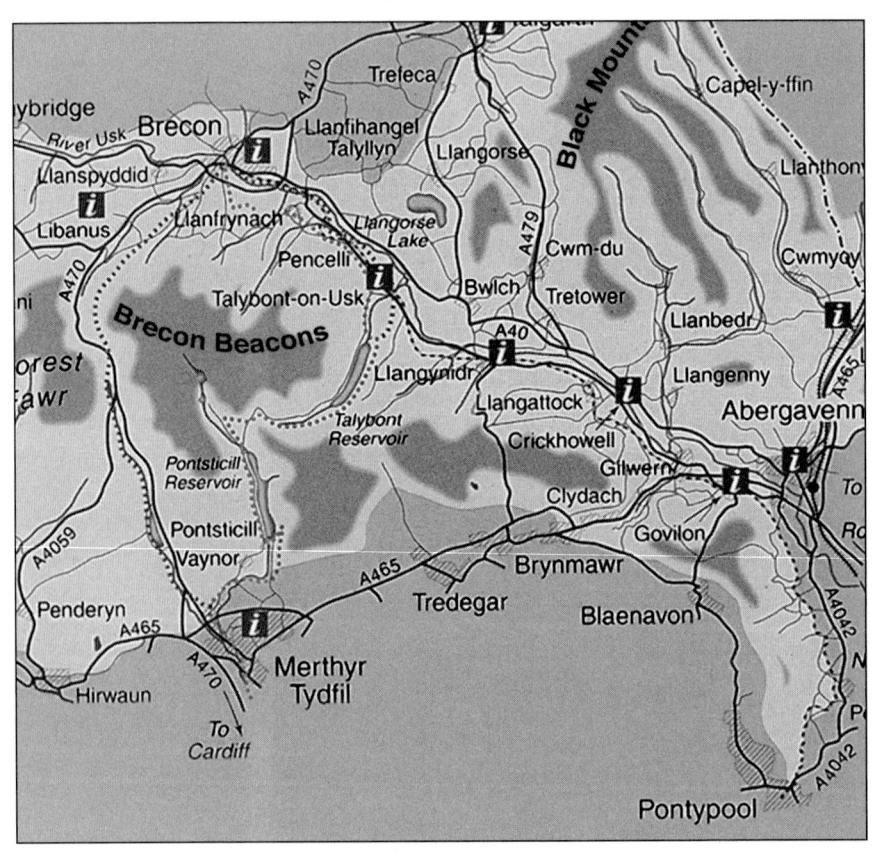

TOUR TWO

THE BRECON BEACONS

BRECON

TALYBONT ON USK

LLANGYNIDR

LLANGATTOCK

GILWERN

CLYDACH GORGE

GOVILON

THE BLORENGE

PONTYPOOL

BLAENAVON

MERTHYR TYDFIL

PONTSTICILL

STOREY ARMS TO PEN Y FAN

FFWDGRECH TO PEN Y FAN

THE BRECON BEACONS TOUR No.1

BRIDGE OVER THE HONDDU AT BRECON
WITH THE CASTLE AND PRIORY

Soft ground etching

Drawn and engraved by J. G. Wood

c. 1811

THE BRECON BEACONS TOUR No.1

BRECON CASTLE & Y GAER

Brecon not only makes a good starting place to make a tour of the Black Mountains area of the National Park, but it is also the ideal starting place for a tour of the impressive Brecon Beacons. From the highest part of the town there are splendid views of **Corn Du, Pen y Fan and Cribyn,** the three highest Beacons.

Whilst in the town of Brecon it is worth taking a look at **Brecon Castle,** which is situated in the grounds of the Castle Hotel just below the cathedral. Unless one is a guest at the hotel one has to be content with viewing the castle from the outside. The castle was built at the end of the eleventh century by Bernard de Newmarch, a distant relative of William the Conqueror, and was originally a simple motte and bailey structure. The walls of this first fortress were partly built with the stones from the old Roman station of **Caerbannau, (Y Gaer),** which was the Welsh capital of Brycheiniog, three miles west of Brecon near Aberyscir. In the twelfth century a polygonal shell was added to the motte, in the thirteenth century a hall and a round tower, and in the fourteenth century a semi-octagonal tower. The castle was regularly attacked by Owain Glyndwr and at that particular time it was in the charge of Sir Thomas Berkeley. Today the castle is in ruins and the most significant structure is the Ely tower, which was once the prison of Bishop Morton of Ely in the reign of Richard III.

From Brecon the tour continues south east, out of the town, along the A40 to the junction with the B4558, where one turns right to the village of Talybont-on-Usk.

'The former metropolis of this district was at Caerbannau, where it continued till the defeat and overthrow of the last British regulus by Bernard Newmarch. The Norman leader demolished the old town, and with the materials, erected, about the year 1094, the Castle of Brecknock, which became afterwards the residence of his successors.'
T.Rees. 1815.

THE BRECON BEACONS TOUR No.2

THE LIME KILNS AT TALYBONT ON USK

An artist's impression of activity around George Overton's lime-kilns, beside the Monmouthshire and Brecon Canal.

Black and white drawing

Miclael Blackmore

2003

Reproduced by kind permission of the Brinore Tramway Conservation Forum 2003

THE BRECON BEACONS TOUR No.2

TALYBONT-ON-USK

Talybont-on-Usk, nestling below the beacons **Waun Rhdd (769m) and Allt Lwyd (654m),** is a popular mooring place on the Monmouthshire and Brecon Canal. In the early 19th century Talybont-on-Usk was an important industrial centre with its own station on the Brecon and Merthyr Railway. It also was the terminus of the Brinore Tramroad as it brought vast quantities of limestone to the vast kilns beside the canal. The remains of these kilns can still be seen today.

At Talybont-on-Usk one can cross the canal and follow the narrow road which leads to the **Talybont Reservoir.** This reservoir is set in a charming wooded valley surrounded by splendid hills. At the far end of the reservoir there are two parking places, which make excellent starting points for **two comparatively easy walks. The first** of these is in the Torpantau forest following the Taff Trail, which is also part of the National Cycle Network route, back to Talybont-on-Usk. **The second** walk is to the many delightful waterfalls that can be seen in the Torpantau area. This walk is clearly marked by different coloured posts and these are explained on a small leaflet which is usually available in the car park. The most spectacular of these waterfalls is known as **Blaen y glyn** on the River Caerfanell which rises high up in the Beacons. After heavy rain these waterfalls can be spectacular, but great care must be taken when walking on the wet rocks.

Having visited this splendid part of the National Park, one returns to Talybont-on-Usk in order to continue the tour of the Brecon Beacons area, via the two villages of Llangynidr and Llangattock.

'The Brecknockshire canal was begun in April 1796, and in December 1800 the first boat-load of coals was brought to Brecon, by that conveyance, from Lllangrunny, near the mouth of the Clydach, a distance of eighteen miles.'
J.G.Wood. 1813.

THE BRECON BEACONS TOUR NO.3

LLANGYNIDIR BRIDGE

Watercolour

From a drawing book by General Roy & Mudge

c. 1821

Reproduced by permission of Llyfrgell Genedlaethol Cymru
The National Library of Wales

THE BRECON BEACONS TOUR No.3

LLANGYNIDR AND LLANGATTOCK

From Talybont-on-Usk the tour continues along the B4558, which runs more or less parallel with the Monmouthshire and Brecon Canal. After a mile or so the canal passes through the 375 yards long **Ashford Tunnel**. It is interesting to note that there is no tow path in the tunnel and so in the days when the narrowboats were horse drawn the horses had to be led over the top and the boats 'legged' or 'shafted' through the tunnel. Today the boats tend to be mechanised and so this curious scene is not too familiar.

After viewing the canal tunnel one eventually comes to the village of **Llangynidr,** lying at the foot of **Mynydd Llangynidr (541m),** which is noted for the large number of 'shake holes', caused by the collapse of the overlying millstone grit into the caves below. At Llangynidr there is a particularly fine four-arched bridge which crosses over a splendid wide stretch of the River Usk.

From Llangynidr the road continues to follow the canal to the village of **Llangattock,** which takes its name from the celtic saint, Cattwg, who lived in St David's time in the sixth century. The parish church still has some of its original twelfth century features, though it was heavily restored in 1885, when the village was a thriving community of weavers and had an active limestone quarrying industry. Above the village is **Mynydd Llangattock, (529m)** which like Mynydd Llangynidr also contains a number of 'shake holes', which explains the former limestone industry here. The limestone escarpment above the village is noted for its cave systems and the Craig y Cilau Nature Reserve.

'Langattock is enlivened by the appearance of a few gentlemen's houses in the neighbourhood, that form pleasing ornaments to the rich and delightful landscape which this spot exhibits. Those more particularly entitled to notice, from the beauty of their situation, and the prospects they command, are Glanwysc, Llangattock Place, Dan y Park and Dan y Graig.'
T.Rees. 1815.

THE BRECON BEACONS TOUR No.4

Abergavenny & Blorenge Mountain, from the Asylum.

ABERGAVENNY & BLORENGE MOUNTAIN
FROM THE ASYLUM

Steel engraving

Engraved by Newman & Co. & published by C. Denton, Abergavenny

c.1870

THE BRECON BEACONS TOUR No.4

GILWERN & THE CLYDACH GORGE,

GOVILON & THE BLORENGE

The Monmouthshire and Brecon Canal continues southwards through **Gilwern,** which lies at the foot of the charming Clydach Gorge. **The Clydach Gorge** today is known as a particularly beautiful area with some interesting walks. However, in the past it was a place of considerable industry and it is still possible to see remains of the former 18th century industrial ironworks. An etching made by J.G.Wood in 1811 gives a good picture of a similar iron works at Llanelly, just a short distance away from Clydach. The reason for this industry in this enchanting gorge was simply due to the fact that it had the natural resources of iron ore, water, wood and coal to hand, all of which were necessary in the manufacture of iron. Today the former industry in the Clydach Gorge has gone and it has become a place of great beauty with fine beech woods, which form part of a National Nature Reserve.

From Gilwern one follows the canal on to **Govilon,** which has become an important centre for the increasing number of canal users and also an excellent place either to view or walk to **the Blorenge (559m).** The Blorenge, like the Clydach Gorge, also has a number of signs of a former industrial past, something that was so prevalent in this particular area of South Wales. Today the Blorenge has become a popular place for the sports of hang gliding and parascending.

'The river Clydach rises in the mountains to the south-west; and rushing with great impetuosity down a rapid descent, forms the picturesque fall of Pwll y Cwn i.e. the Dogs' Pool, so called from a tradition of the murdered body of a woman being there discovered almost eaten by dogs. There was another fall at the upper end of this romantic valley, called Pistill–Mawr, or the Great Spout, which was destroyed by the opening of coal works some time since.'
J.G.Wood. 1813.

THE BRECON BEACONS TOUR No.5

IRON WORKS AT BLAENAVON

Copper engraving

Drawn by Sir Richard Hoare and engraved by W.Byrne

c. 1800

THE BRECON BEACONS TOUR No.5

PONTYPOOL & BLAENAVON

It may seem strange that the Brecon Beacons National Park appears to extend southwards to **Pontypool,** like a miniature Italy. The reason for this is that Pontypool was close to the junction of the Brecknock and Abergavenny canal with the Monmouthshire canal, which met at Pontymoile. Also Pontypool was a very important iron and tinplate making town and this industrial past is now skillfully remembered in the Valley Inheritance Museum, housed in the former Georgian stables in Pontypool Park.

About six miles north west of Pontypool the tour continues to the former industrial town of **Blaenavon,** famous for both its ironworks and for its colliery. The iron works were a milestone in the history of the Industrial Revolution, for they were the first purpose-built multi-furnace ironworks in Wales, and were established here in 1788-89. By 1796 Blaenavon was the second largest ironworks in Wales producing 5,400 tons of iron a year. These furnaces were eventually closed in 1904, but thanks to local initiative and CADW one can still view much of the works site, including its impressive water balance tower.

Blaenavon was also well known for its colliery, which like most of the other South Wales collieries was closed in 1980. However, it was soon afterwards reopened to the public as the Big Pit Mining Museum where one can view the former coal mining industry both above ground and 300 ft. underground. Blaenavon's historic iron and coal mining history was recognized in 2000 when the town was declared an UNESCO World Heritage Site.

'The manufacture of tin and iron is carried on extensively throughout the district, and so rapidly have these sources of employment extended, that the population of the parish [Pontypool], which in 1802 was only 1,472, amounted to 18,146 in 1871.'
Black's Picturesque Guide to South Wales. 1874.

THE BRECON BEACONS TOUR No.6

CYFARTHA IRON WORKS.

CYFARTHA IRON WORKS

Soft ground etching

Drawn & engraved by J.G.Wood

c. 1811

THE BRECON BEACONS TOUR No.6

MERTHYR TYDFIL & PONTSTICILL

The southern boundary of the National Park runs more or less parallel with the A465, known as the Heads of the Valleys Road. So, strictly speaking, **Merthyr Tydfil** is just outside the Park. Even so it is right to include in the tour *'the former iron and steel capital of the world'*. This great industry began in 1759 when John Guest's Dowlais Ironworks were opened, followed in 1765 by the Crawshay's massive works at Cyfartha and even more foundries in 1767 and in 1784. The extension of the Monmouthshire canal from Merthyr to Cardiff was also a great boost to the industry, as were the tramway in 1802, and Brunel's railway to Cardiff in 1841. By 1831 the population of Merthyr was more than the combined populations of Cardiff, Swansea and Newport! The industrial decline came early in the 20th century, largely due to the importing of cheaper ore from abroad. Merthyr's former industrial prestige is now recalled in the Ynysfach Iron Heritage Centre, housed in a 19th century engine house. An example of the wealth of the powerful ironmasters can be seen at mock gothic Cyfartha Castle, built as the home for the Crawshay family, and now a museum and art gallery.

Three miles north of Merthyr is Pant Station, the home of **the Brecon Mountain Railway.** This narrow gauge steam railway runs along the bed of the former Brecon and Merthyr Railway of 1859-1962. From Pant Station the train follows the eastern side of the attractive **Pontsticill Reservoir** to Dol-y-Gaer, where there are marvellous views both of the reservoir and of the Brecon Beacons. Pontsticill Reservoir was completed in 1927 and was the last in a chain of four releasing some 6.5 million gallons of water daily. On the other side of the reservoir walkers can pick up the Taff Trail, which crosses the Beacons on its way to Brecon.

'Enveloped as this place [Merthyr] is perpetually in smoke, and stunned by the constant din of the forges, the neighbourhood cannot be supposed adapted to furnish any gentlemen's houses, beside those which pertain to the proprietors of the works, whose first consideration would be convenience.'
T.Rees. 1815.

THE BRECON BEACONS TOUR No.7

THE BRECON BEACONS

Watercolour

From a drawing book by General Roy & Mudge

c. 1821

Reproduced by permission of Llyfrgell Genedlaethol Cymru
The National Library of Wales

THE BRECON BEACONS TOUR No.7

TWO ROUTES TO PEN Y FAN

The highest and most distinctive of all the Beacons is **Pen y Fan** and there are many approaches to this splendid mountain. For the purpose of this tour these have been limited to two. **The first** and most popular route is from **Storey Arms** on the A470 trunk road from Brecon to Cardiff. Storey Arms is an outdoor–pursuits centre and is named after the inn that used to be near the present day car park. The path to Pen y Fan is clearly marked and is a fairly easy walk. However some people are put off by having to cross Blaen-Taf-Fawr, which has a series of attractive cascades, near the start of the walk. As one approaches the summit one arrives first at Corn Du (873m) and then on to Pen y Fan (886m). The views here, on a clear day, are absolutely superb, for one can have a panoramic view of the whole of the Brecon Beacons National Park.

The second walk to Pen y Fan is from the village of **Ffwdgrech,** south west of Brecon, where one more or less follows **Cwm Llwch.** This is a much more attractive route to Pen y Fan, but is steeper towards the summit. Beyond Ffwdgrech is a fine waterfall at Pont Ryrd Goch *(Bridge of the Red Ford),* which in season has a wonderful display of foxgloves, these may have given the name to the fall. Further up the cwm there are a number of other small falls, which are enhanced by the bright red berries of the Rowan trees. Then, as one begins the steep ascent to Pen y Fan, one can look down on the mysterious glacial lake, Llyn Cwm Llwch. Just below Corn Du, one passes the memorial stone to the five year old Tommy Jones. In 1900 Tommy Jones was found dead on this spot, having become separated from his father on a visit to his grandparents in Cwm Llwch. This tragedy acts as a solemn reminder today of the possible dangers that the elements can present to any walker of the Beacons.

'Although apparently only about two miles distant [from Brecon] I found the ascent occupied several hours of persevering exertion I branched off to the left passing through the opening between the hills called Cwm-llwch, to the summit of the highest eminence. The scene was indescribably grand.'
T.Roscoe. c.1837.

TOUR THREE
FFOREST FAWR

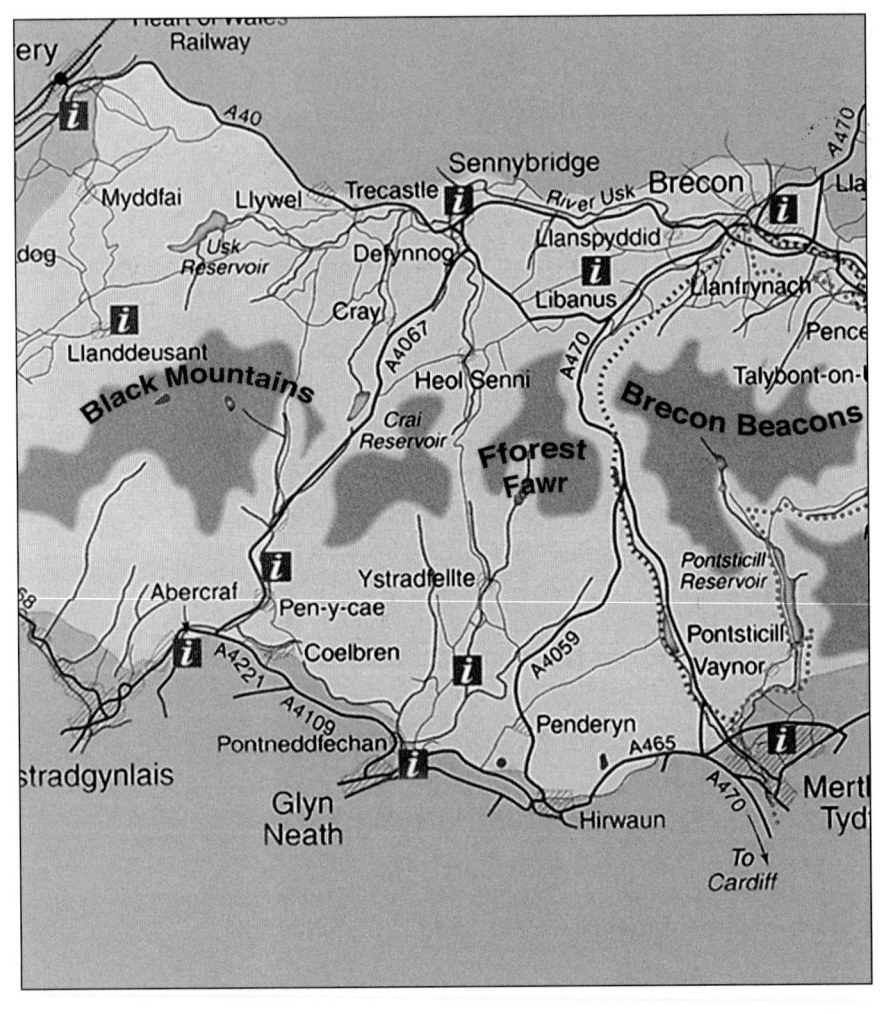

TOUR THREE

FFOREST FAWR

BRECON BRIDGE &

BRECON FRIARY

LIBANUS

PONTNEDDFECHAN

RIVERS PYRDDIN & NEDD

CRAIG Y DDINAS

SYCHRYD GORGE &

BWA MAEN

COELBREN

HENRHYD FALL

RIVERS MELLTE & HEPSTE

PORTH YR OGOF

YSTRADFELLTE

MAEN LLIA

THE FFOREST FAWR TOUR No.1

BRECON BRIDGE

Copper engraving

Drawn by G. Samuel and engraved by J. Storer

c. 1798

THE FFOREST FAWR TOUR No.1

BRECON BRIDGE, FRIARY & LIBANUS

Brecon made a good starting place for both the Black Mountains Tour and for the Brecon Beacons Tour, and it is also a convenient place to begin the third tour of Fforest Fawr, the area west of the Brecon Beacons and east of the Black Mountain.

Brecon as well as having a cathedral church (cf p.4) and a castle (cf p.42) also has a fine **bridge** spanning the Honddu just below the castle before it joins the Usk in the town. Near to the junction of these two rivers can be seen the remains of a former **Dominican Friary,** founded in 1250. The Friary was revived, in the nineteenth century, as Christ's College, which now uses the re-roofed friary choir as its college chapel.

About six miles south west of Brecon, just off the A470 road, is the National Park's excellent Visitor Centre at **Libanus.** The visitor centre has been built on the ancient common of Mynydd Illtud, named after the Celtic missionary St Illtud, who like St David, was a great Christian influence in Wales. Tradition states that St Illtud was buried near the road to the north of the Visitor Centre and the site is marked by a collection of stones in a shallow hollow.

The National Park Visitor Centre at Libanus makes an excellent place to visit before undertaking any tour of the Beacons, as there are experts on hand who can give sound advice about walking, cycling or driving in the Park. It also has a lecture room, a good bookshop and a refreshment room, with superb views over the common to the Beacons and Fforest Fawr. Altogether it makes a splendid place to spend a relaxed morning or afternoon, either before or after a walk in this beautiful part of Wales.

'Christ Church College is situated on the banks of the Usk, at a short distance from the bridge. The history of the original foundation at this place is not known. It is ascertained to have been a monastery of Black Friars, with an appurtenant church dedicated to St Nicholas'.
T.Rees. 1815.

THE FFOREST FAWR TOUR No.2

PORTNEATH, VAUGHN

(Pontneddfechan)

Sepia aquatint

Artist and Engraver not known

c. 1795

THE FFOREST FAWR TOUR No.2

PONTNEDDFECHAN

From the National Park Visitor Centre at Libanus one has quite a long journey to the more popular southern part of Fforest Fawr. From Libanus one takes the A470 south, with Fan Fawr (734m) on the right. At the junction of the A470 & A4059 one takes the A4059 to Penderyn, with Moel Penderyn (371m) on the right. Finally from Penderyn one joins the Heads of the Valleys Road to get to the village of Pontneddfechan from Glyn Neath.

Pontneddfechan, as the name implies, is the bridge over the River Nedd. However, it is really the junction of five rivers, all of which have their sources high up in Fforest Fawr and have a series of most dramatic waterfalls, which go to make superb walks in this waterfall area. The falls that one can visit from Pontneddfechan are those on the River Nedd and on the River Pyrddin, which joins the Nedd about a mile above Pontneddfechan bridge.

There are two named falls on the **Pyrddin.** The first is called **Sgwd Gwladys,** a fall of about forty feet, and, because of a geological fault, the river flows mainly on the left-hand side of the rocks. This charming fall is very accessible as it is close to the confluence of the two rivers. The second fall, **Sgwd Einion Gam,** is further up the river, and quite difficult to find as it involves crossing the river several times in order to reach a fine fall of about seventy feet.

There are three exciting falls on the **Nedd,** all of which are comparatively easy to reach. The first is called the **Horseshoe Falls,** so named because of their distinctive shape, the second is called **Lower Sgwd Ddwli,** which is a two stage fall, and the third **Upper Sgwd Ddwll,** a particularly fine wide fall and making a fitting return point for the walk back to Pontneddfechan.

'The village of Pont Neath Faughan stands at the head of the valley, at the confluence of five rivers, each of them contributing its rocks, woods, and waterfalls, to the general grandeur and magnificence which here seem brought to a focus.'
Jones's South Wales Illustrated. 1830.

THE FFOREST FAWR TOUR No.3

CRAIG Y DINAS

Steel engraving

Drawn by H. Gastineau and engraved by W.Radclyffe

c. 1830

THE FFOREST FAWR TOUR No.3

CRAIG Y DINAS & BWA MAEN

About a mile north east of Pontneddfechan one comes to **Craig y Dinas,** a huge, precipitous, limestone rock which rises very steeply for about 200 feet, and now a popular venue for those who want to learn the art of rock climbing. From the top of Craig y Dinas there is a superb view down the whole of the Vale of Neath, an area that had such an attraction for the artist William Weston Young, who drew a whole series of coloured etchings of the Vale in 1835. Immediately below Craig y Dinas lies the **Sychryd Gorge,** where the River Sychryd joins the River Mellte just before it meets the Nedd at Pontneddfechan. In this valley there are substantial remains of the former silica mining industry that thrived here in the 19th century. At the far end of this valley there is an impressive waterfall, which still has obvious signs that it had been used to power the industrial machinery that used to be used in this attractive valley.

Close to Craig y Dinas, on the River Sychryd, is a large, curious arch shaped limestone rock called **Bwa Maen,** or the Stone Bow. This rock is about ninety feet high and seventy feet wide and its base has been washed absolutely smooth by the river as it flows beside the rock. Underneath the curving overhang is a narrow entrance to a cave known locally as Y Ffwrn or the Oven. The limestone from this area used to be very much sought after in the 19th century in order to create fashionable imitation marble mantelpieces in London.

'After passing Pontneddfecchan, the Dinas rock, rising abruptly among the surrounding mountains, is a grand and pleasing object. The view is taken a little below the bridge. You ascend the rock by a narrow and steep road; on the summit you cannot help being struck with an object just at your feet, the Marquis of Bute's beautiful nursery; from which have sprung the fine plantations of larch &c. clothing the hills and slopes around.'
William Weston Young. 1835.

THE FFOREST FAWR TOUR No.4

HENRHYD FALL

Sepia watercolour

Drawn by W.W. Young

c. 1830

Reproduced by kind permission of the
National Museums & Galleries of Wales

THE FFOREST FAWR TOUR No.4

COELBREN & HENRHYD FALL

From Craig y Ddinas the tour returns to Glyn Neath, where one takes the A4109 to **Coelbren.** Just south of Coelbren one crosses the site of the former Roman road, known as Sarn Helen, which linked the Roman fort of Nidium, near Neath, with Y Gaer, near Brecon. From Coelbren it is possible to follow the route of this Roman road through Fforest Fawr more or less all the way to the National Park Visitor Centre at Mynydd Illtud.

Close to Coelbren can be seen the magnificent waterfall known as **Henrhyd Waterfall.** This fall is now in the care of the National Trust, who have made access to the fall so much easier by providing a steep twisting path. From the bottom of the fall one can look up and see the River Llech tumble ninety feet over the ledge in a single fall. The River Llech is only a very tiny river, but after heavy rain or snow it does produce this really splendid fall on its way to join the River Tawe.

Coelbren used to be a centre of a vast open-cast coal mining industry, which makes this particular part of the National Park a rather depressing area with all its very obvious signs of surface coal mining. However, it is interesting to see the seam of coal, which runs clearly behind Henrhyd Fall.

From Coelbren the tour returns the way it came to Glyn Neath, where one takes the Pontneddfechan road towards the small village of Ystradfellte, making a good starting point to visit the falls on the Rivers Mellte and Hepste.

'Henrhyd and its coal works are in an elevated situation, about two miles eastward of the Tawe, from whence a great quantity of coal is sent down the Swansea Canal; almost the whole of which was conveyed by the Neath Canal, before that of Swansea was formed.'
J.G.Wood 1817.

THE FFOREST FAWR TOUR No.5

UPPER & LOWER FALLS OF THE HEPTSE

Steel engraving

Drawn by H. Gastineau and engraved by S. Lacey

c. 1830

THE FFOREST FAWR TOUR No.5

FALLS ON THE MELLTE & HEPSTE

About two miles north of Pontneddfechan, on the right of the narrow road, is a large lay by. This makes a good place to park a car and to begin the exciting walk to five named waterfalls, on two rivers, both of which have their source high up in Fforest Fawr.

The first river one meets is the **River Mellte** on which there are three fine falls. The first is **Sgwd Clyn-gwyn.** This is a two step fall dropping first onto a rocky ledge, with a subsequent fall of about 50 feet. The second fall is called **Sgwd Isaf Clyn-gwyn.** This is a particularly spectacular fall, which descends for about twenty feet in a curtain of water over a steep ledge. It then swings round at an angle dropping another forty feet into the gorge below. The third fall on the Mellte is **Sgwd y Pannwr.** This fall has been created by a tilt in the rock strata, which causes the river to flow to one side of the valley, and producing three graceful falls.

Shortly after visiting Sgwd y Pannwr one meets the confluence of the River Mellte with the **River Hepste,** on which there are two more splendid falls. The first is the **Lower Cilhepste.** This is really a whole succession of cascades, which drop dramatically for about three hundred and fifty feet through a narrow ravine. The second fall is known as **Sgwd yr Eira** and is probably the best known of all the falls in this area. The popular appeal of this particular fall is largely due to the fact one can walk behind it. Over the centuries the heavy spray from the fall has eroded the soft shale behind it, creating a natural path to the other side of the river, and providing an alternative approach to the falls from the village of Penderyn.

'The effect of the sun shining upon the cascade [Sgwd yr Eira] on a fine day, seen from behind, the sparkling of the water, and vivid brightness of everything without, contrasted with the sombre colour of the rock and black pool below, is singularly impressive.'
J.G.Wood. 1811.

THE FFOREST FAWR TOUR No.6

PORTH YR OGOF

Sepia watercolour

Drawn by W. W. Young

c. 1830

Reproduced by kind permission of the
National Museums & Galleries of Wales

THE FFOREST FAWR TOUR NO.6

PORTH YR OGOF & YSTRADFELLTE

After visiting the splendid falls on the Mellte and Hepste one returns to the minor road, which goes to Ystradfellte, where there is another place of great interest to visit. This is impressive entrance to **Porth yr Ogof,** where the River Mellte goes underground for nearly three-quarters of a mile. The entrance to the cave is one of the largest in Wales and is a favourite venue for experienced cavers. The bed of the River Mellte is usually dry here, but after heavy rain, it can quickly become a raging torrent. Only those who have a good knowledge of the cave should go any distance inside, for it can present all sorts of dangers. There is a passage to the right of the main entrance, which leads to a remarkable cavern of about 6000 square feet. The ceiling of this immense cavern is completely flat and has no means of support other than the sides of the cave. The river emerges again half a mile upstream at the Blue Pool.

From Porth yr Ogof one quickly comes to the tiny village of **Ystradfellte,** with its small church and a public house, and out into the heart of Fforest Fawr. It is here that one is more conscious of the superb open countryside with **Fan Nedd (663m)** on the left and **Fan Llia (614m)** on the right. Between these two mountains and fairly close to the road is the massive 12ft Neolithic/early Bronze Age standing stone, known as **Maen Llia.** The road then follows a series of alarming hairpin bends presenting one with a fine panoramic view down the Senni valley and on to **Sennybridge,** which will be the starting point of the final tour.

'We penetrated [Porth yr Ogof] about one hundred yards, as far as any glimmering of day light from the mouth directed us; and this specimen of stygian horror was amply sufficient to satisfy all rational curiosity. There is a passage to the right where it is necessary to take candles, which having pursued for a short way, you come to a very considerable area, excavated to a great height, and partially illuminated by an aperture at the top. The effect is most striking and stupendous.'
Jones's South Wales Illustrated. 1830.

TOUR FOUR

THE BLACK MOUNTAIN

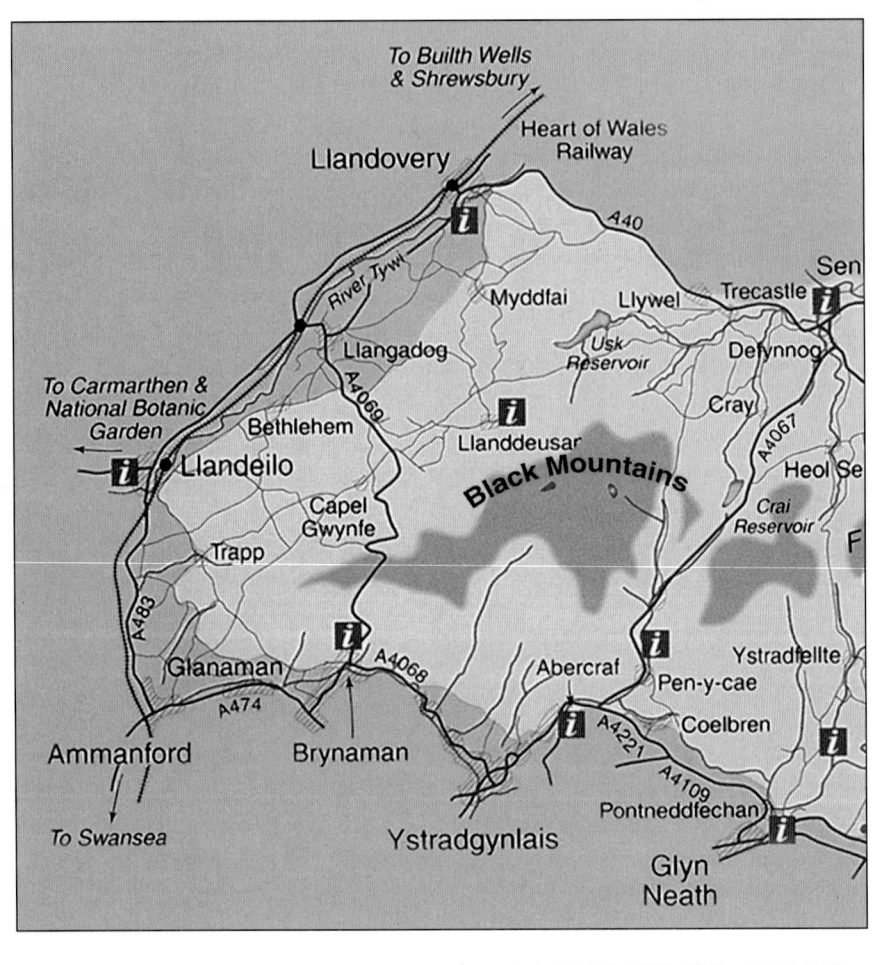

TOUR FOUR
THE BLACK MOUNTAIN

SENNYBRIDGE

DEFYNNOG & MAEN MAWR

DAN YR OGOF

CRAIG- Y-NOS & SAITH MAEN

SOURCE OF THE LOUGHOR

CARREG CENNEN

LLANDEILO

DINEFWR PARK

CARN GOCH

THE BLACK MOUNTAIN

LLANDOVERY

Y PIGWN & ROMAN ROAD

TRECASTLE

THE BLACK MOUNTAIN TOUR No.1

SOURCE OF THE TAWE

(Near Cerrig Duon & Maen Mawr)

Soft ground etching

Drawn & etched by J.G. Wood

c. 1813

THE BLACK MOUNTAIN TOUR No.1

SENNYBRIDGE, DEFYNNOG & MAEN MAWR

The final tour of the Brecon Beacons National Park begins at Sennybridge and covers the area surrounding **the Black Mountain** or Bannau Sir Gaer (749m) and Fan Brycheiniog (802m). **Sennybridge,** on the old mail coach road (now the main A40 trunk road from Brecon to Llandeilo), takes its name from the bridge over Afon Senni. The small market town has the remains of a 13th century Welsh castle, known as Castell Du, built on the western banks of Afon Senni and looking southwards to Fforest Fach (381m). Castell Du was never properly completed and it only has a simple round tower attached to a small domestic block. Today the remains of the castle have been neglected and are surrounded by a number of modern houses, which tend to obscure the view of the castle.

South of Sennybridge is the village of **Defynnog,** once a busy agricultural and rural craft centre and boasting in having no less than twenty shoemakers working here at the same time! Today the chief interest lies in the 15th century church, which can trace its origins back to the 5th century. A curious feature is a 5th or 6th century stone with a Latin inscription built into the south-west corner of the tower. Also, inside the church, there is a 12th century font with a strange ancient Anglo-Saxon or Runic inscription, thought to be the only reversed Runic inscription in Wales.

The tour of the Black Mountain continues along the A4067, passing Cray Reservoir and Bwlch Bryn-rhudd (369m), to the minor road on the right, which follows the Tawe valley. After two miles one comes to the curious prehistoric stone oval of **Cerrig Duon,** a rare shape, of which there are only ten examples in Britain. Close to the stone oval there is the fine standing stone known as **Maen Mawr.**

'Near the road [in] the vale of Tawe some druidical remains, called Cerig duon, or the Black Stones, may be seen, and the pass near them is called Bwlch y Cerig duon; they resemble circles of stones at St Clare's, in Cornwall, except that a stone much larger than the rest is there wanting.'
J.G.Wood. 1813.

THE BLACK MOUNTAIN TOUR No.2

CRAIG-Y-NOS CASTLE

Woodcut from sketches reproduced in the Graphic

November 24th 1888

Reproduced by kind permission of Brecknock Museum & Art Gallery

THE BLACK MOUNTAIN TOUR No.2

DAN YR OGOF & CRAIG-Y-NOS

The tour continues along the A4067 to Glyntawe, near Abercraf, where there are two major tourist attractions. The first of these attractions are the spectacular caves known as the **Dan yr Ogof Caves**. The caves were first discovered in 1912, but the full extent of their complex system was not realized for another twenty years. Today Dan yr Ogof has been chosen as the National Showcaves Centre for Wales, for there are at least ten miles of known passages and experienced cavers confidently believe that there are still many other undiscovered passages. The public have access to just three of these caves. The first is the original showcave with its narrow passageways, stalactites and stalagmites, the second is the high impressive Cathedral Cave and the third is Ogof yr Esgryn or the Bone Cave, which interprets the archaeology and history of the area.

The second attraction, on the other side of the road, is the **Craig-y-nos Country Park**. This is set in the former the pleasure grounds of the ornate Craig-y-nos Castle built in 1878, by the internationally famous opera singer Madame Adelina Patti. Here the opera singer would entertain her guests from all over the world in great style and even built a small theatre, based on the design of the Drury Lane Theatre in London. The castle is in private ownership and is only on view from time to time, but the picturesque 40 acres of the Country Park, with its river meadows, grassland, woodlands, lake and ornamental features, is open every day.

High above and to the west of the Country Park is another interesting set of prehistoric stones known as **Saith Maen**. This is an alignment of seven stones, which interestingly point towards Cerrig Duon, an oval of twenty stones. (see p.69)

'Southward the deepening valley descends to copper-works and Swansea, and immediately below us – an oasis – are the turrets, gardens, and green terraces of Craig-y-Nos, the strangely chosen residence of Mme. Adelina Patti.'
Thorough Guide Series. 1901.

THE BLACK MOUNTAIN TOUR No.3

CARREG CENNEN CASTLE

Wood engraving

Drawn & engraved by H. Hughes

c. 1823

THE BLACK MOUNTAIN TOUR No.3

THE LOUGHOR & CARREG CENNEN

From Abercraf the tour continues on the western side of the Black Mountain. This initially involves a number of main roads to Glanaman, where one turns right at the minor road to Trapp and Llandeilo, following the boundary of the National Park.

At Dre-Fach the minor road crosses the **River Loughor,** whose source, about two miles upstream, flows out of a cavern situated just below **Tair Carn Uchaf (482m)** and **Tair Carn Isaf (460m).** The Loughor is a particularly charming small river and has a splendid waterfall further downstream in the grounds of Glynhir Mansion, just outside the National Park.

At the village of Trapp one can follow the CADW signs for the dramatic **Carreg Cennen Castle,** set on top of a 90 metre high limestone crag, commanding a superb view over the surrounding countryside. Originally Carreg Cennen was a Welsh castle, but in 1277 it was captured by the troops of Edward I and then granted to John Giffard. Most of the surviving buildings date back to the late 13th and early 14th century. In 1287 there was a Welsh revolt and the castle passed to the Earl of Hereford and the inner ward has many marks of this period. Carreg Cennen is similar in design to many of the castles built in North Wales by Edward I, where one set of defences was built inside another. A curious feature at Carreg Cennen is the 30 yard, narrow vaulted tunnel, along the cliff face leading to a natural cave, used in part as a dovecote and also as a lookout against attacks from below. In the 19th century the Cawdor family carried out very extensive restoration work, which is clearly seen in the newer blue-grey stone and by the white deposits on this stone from the lime that was used for the mortar.

'The castle of Caraig-cennin is most strongly situated on the point of a high, craggy, insulated rock, three sides of which are wholly inaccessible: It is surrounded at moderate, but unequal, distances, with mountains, and the roads to it are, even now, but barely practicable.'
H.P.Wyndham. 1781.

THE BLACK MOUNTAIN TOUR No.4

DINEFOR CASTLE

Soft ground etching

Drawn and etched by J. G. Wood

c. 1812

THE BLACK MOUNTAIN TOUR No.4

LLANDEILO & DINEFWR

From Carreg Cennen one returns to Trapp and takes the road towards Llandeilo, an excellent centre for various attractions in the Vale of Tywi, as well as having good views toward the Black Mountain. The pleasant town of **Llandeilo,** just outside the National Park, is set high above the River Tywi and takes its name from St Teilo, who is thought to have founded a monastery here in 560, and the Parish Church has been dedicated to his honour.

On the western side of Llandeilo is the large **Dinefwr Park,** created in 18th century by great landscape designer Capability Brown and now managed by the National Trust. Within the park can be seen the White Park Cattle, a rare bred of cattle that have been associated with Dinefwr for over 900 years. Dinefwr also has three types of fallow deer; the black, the brown and the mottled, which often are seen grazing in the park. At the entrance to Dinefwr Park is **Newton House,** a 17th century house, which was substantially altered and re-faced with limestone in the 19th century. In 1990 the National Trust bought the rapidly deteriorating property and since then have carried out a major restoration programme and the house is now is open to the public.

At the far end of the park, standing proud in a strategic position high above the Tywi valley, is **Dinefwr Castle.** This has been a fortified site since the Iron Age and a castle may have been built as early as 877. Soon afterwards it became the court of Hywel Dda, the ruler of much of South West Wales and Gwynedd. The present castle dates back to the early 12th century, when Rhys ap Gruffydd was the ruler of South West Wales. Recently CADW have carried out a comprehensive restoration plan, which enables visitors to have a much better impression of the original castle built on this dramatic site.

'The ruins of Dinevawr Castle stand on the lofty prominence of a beautiful semicircular hill, entirely mantled with wood, and which, with a regular sweep. precipitately descends to the Towy.'
H.P.Wyndham. 1781.

THE BLACK MOUNTAIN TOUR No.5

LLYN Y FACH & THE BLACK MOUNTAIN

Photograph

Original coloured photograph by Jeremy Moore

Reproduced by kind permission of Jeremy Moore

THE BLACK MOUNTAIN TOUR No.5

CARN GOCH & THE BLACK MOUNTAIN

From Llandeilo it is convenient to make a detour to Carn Goch and the Black Mountain and these are both best approached from **Llangadog.** Three miles south of Llangadog is **Carn Goch,** one of the largest Iron Age hillforts in Wales, covering an area of 30 acres. Its massive defences are full of the original stones from the collapsed ramparts and these clearly indicate the fort's former gateways and ditches.

The easiest way to **the Black Mountain** is to carry on along the road from Llangadog and to follow the minor roads to the remote village of **Llanddeusant.** Here there is a small medieval church that has been built on the site of an earlier monastery, which tradition says was founded by St Paulinus, the tutor of St David. The evidence for the church's ancient origin is largely due to the discovery here of a 7th century slab cross.

Llanddeusant village is popular for both climbers and walkers to **Bannau Sir Gaer (749m)** and **Fan Brycheiniog (802m), the** highest point on the Black Mountain. From the village there is an easy and rewarding walk along a stony track to the beautiful **Llyn y Fan Fach,** which nestles comfortably below the dramatic escarpment of Bannau Sir Gaer, and is the gateway to this almost unknown part of the Black Mountain. The three major rivers, the Usk, Tawe and Twrch, all have their source below the highest point of the mountain. An alternative approach to the Black Mountain is from Bwlch Cerrig Duon (see p.69) and this route passes the other attractive mountain lake known as Llyn y Fan Fawr.

'The Usk rises from three springs in a wild and cheerless tract, immediately under the northern side of the highest point of the Black Mountain, or Caermarthenshire Van; about five miles from Trecastle, three from Talsarn [Llanddeusant], and not far from the head of the Twrch river, which separates Glamorganshire from Brecknockshire.'
J.G.Wood. 1811.

THE BLACK MOUNTAIN TOUR No.6

LLANDOVERY CASTLE

Soft ground etching

Drawn and etched by J. G. Wood

c. 1811